# Baby Animals
# LAMB

 Angela Royston

Chrysalis Children's Books

First published in the UK in 2004 by

Chrysalis Children's Books
An imprint of Chrysalis Books Group PLC
The Chrysalis Building, Bramley Road, London W10 6SP

ISBN  1 84458 086 5

British Library Cataloguing in Publication Data
for this book is available from the British Library.

Editorial Manager: Joyce Bentley
Editor: Clare Lewis

Produced by Bender Richardson White
Project Editor: Lionel Bender
Designer: Ben White
Production: Kim Richardson
Picture Researcher: Cathy Stastny
Cover Make-up: Mike Pilley, Radius

Printed in China

10 9 8 7 6 5 4 3 2 1

Words in **bold** can be found in New words on page 31.

**Picture credits**
Corbis Images Inc: Michael St. Maur 27.
Ecoscene: Angela Hampton 7, 9, 10, 14, 17; Sally Morgan 12; Anthony Harrison 13; Pat Jerrold 20;
Chinch Gryniewicz 22; Vicki Coombs 24; Anthony Cooper 26; Sea Spring Photos 28.
Natural History Photo Agency: Susanne Danegger 21; Geoff Bryant 23.
Oxford Scientific Films: Hans Reinhard 29.
Rex Features Ltd: 8; David Hartley 11.
RSPCA Photolibrary: 5; Angela Hampton cover, 4, 6; S Thompson 1, 16; E A Janes 2, 18, 19, 25;
Susan Pitts 15.

NOTE
In this book, we have used photographs of different types of lambs and adult sheep. Each type has wool of a certain colour and pattern.

# Contents

# Just born

This lamb has just been born.
It is wet and tired.

The mother sheep licks her lamb until its **wool** is dry.

# One hour old

The lamb's legs are very **wobbly**. The lamb stands up but quickly falls over.

The mother sheep **nuzzles** it to make it stand up again.

# Feeding

Another lamb has been born. The two lambs feed on their mother's milk.

This lamb is very hungry!
It sucks milk from one of
its mother's **teats**.

# Two days old

The lambs' legs are strong now. They follow their mother wherever she goes.

If one lamb gets left behind, he **bleats** until his mother comes back for him.

# One week old

The lambs feed on grass as well as milk. They cut the grass with their front teeth.

The mother spends most of the day **grazing** with other sheep. She also looks after the lambs.

# Two weeks old

The lambs are becoming braver. They love to **explore**.

This lamb is jumping in the air to strengthen its legs and to have fun.

# Four weeks old

The lambs are growing bigger. But they are still much smaller than their mother.

Their wool starts to grow thick. The farmer marks each lamb by painting a number on its wool.

# Playing

Lambs love to jump and to play. These lambs are standing on their mother's back!

The lambs play together
but they still keep close to
their mother.

# Eight weeks old

The lambs move further away from their mother now. Brother and sister lambs keep together.

They run around all over the field. They walk up hills and jump off **mounds**.

# Four months old

The lambs are growing fast. Look how this lamb is now almost as big as its mother.

In the next few weeks, their wool becomes much thicker and longer.

# Chewing the cud

The lambs spend more time eating now. They chew the grass with their flat back teeth.

Often, they swallow some grass then bring it back to their mouth to chew again. The half-chewed grass is called **cud**.

# Keeping together

Sometimes the farmer and his **sheepdog** move the sheep and lambs to a new field.

The dog collects the sheep and guides them through the gate.

# Six months old

The lambs are now fully grown. They are as big as their mother!

They live with all the other sheep in the **flock**.

# Quiz

1 How many lambs does the mother sheep have?

2 Why does a newborn lamb keep falling over?

3 How does a sheepdog help the farmer?

4 How old are the lambs when they are fully grown?

5 What is cud?

6 What is the name for a group of sheep?

7 At what age do lambs become adults?

8 What does a farmer use to help him move his lambs and sheep round the farm?

The answers are all in this book!

# New words

**bleat** noise made by a sheep or lamb.

**cud** half-chewed grass that a sheep or cow brings back into its mouth from its stomach to chew again.

**explore** to find out for oneself.

**flock** group of sheep that live together.

**graze** to feed on grass in a field.

**mound** little hill or bump in the ground.

**nuzzle** nudge with one's nose.

**teat** part of a mother's body from which her babies suck milk.

**wobbly** shaky.

**wool** thick hair that covers a sheep's and lamb's body.

# Index